It's a Gift

Written by Claire Llewellyn

Contents

Make a gift

This book shows you how to make two gifts.

snake bookmark

pencil dinosaur

Pencil dinosaur

black pen

glue stick

scissors

pencil

thick kitchen cloths

3

1. Fold a cloth in half.

2. Put the pencil on it.

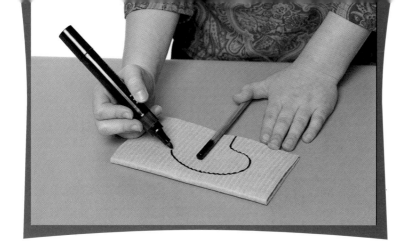

3. Draw a dinosaur head shape around it.

4. Cut out two dinosaur heads.

5

5 Draw and cut out
dinosaur spikes.

6 Stick the spikes on to
one dinosaur head.

7 Put the glue around the other dinosaur head.

8 Stick the other dinosaur head on top.

9 Cut out and draw
cloth eyes and teeth.

10 Stick them on each side.

11 When your dinosaur
is dry, put it on the
end of a pencil.

8

Snake bookmark

You will need:

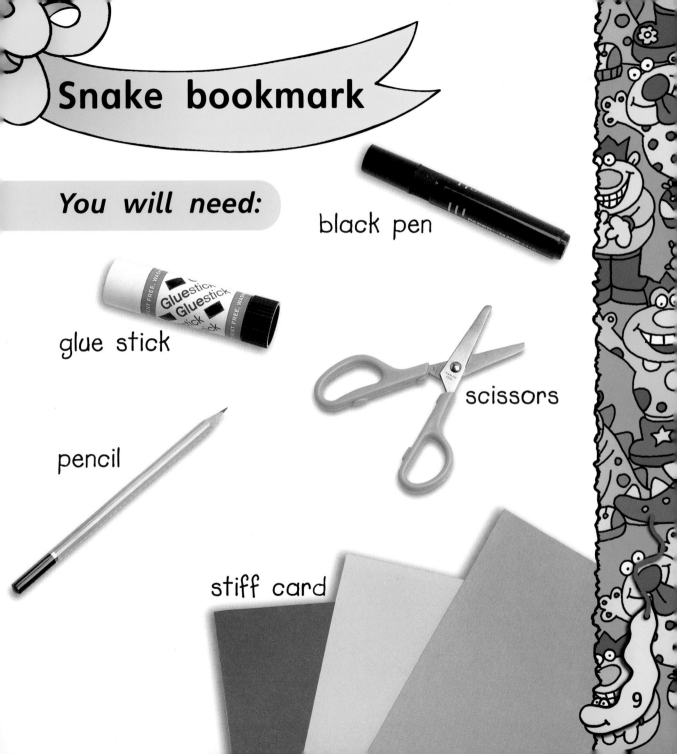

black pen

glue stick

pencil

scissors

stiff card

What to do:

1 Draw a wiggly snake on the card.

2 Cut out the snake.

3 Cut out two eyes and some shapes.

4 Stick the shapes on the snake.

You can make these pencil pets and animal bookmarks too!